GW01464239

EXETER STAINED GLASS
FOREWORD

Stained and painted glass has for over a thousand years transformed the light and atmosphere which enters religious buildings in this country and throughout the continent. It has effectively put colour to the Bible and our well known Gospel stories. The early years saw this as a way of teaching the Bible to those less well versed, as well as edifying the Church to the glory of God. This in turn gives a real appreciation of the works and skills of the craftsmen and women down the ages who created these beautiful works of art.

Exeter Cathedral has a great historical collection of stained and painted glass, much documented in the Cathedral Archives. Up until now there has been no overall guide to this wonderful collection of stained and painted glass, readily accessible to worshippers and visitors.

Examples are glass dating from the 14th century in the Great East Window, by Master Walter and Robert Lyen through to the mid 18th century enamel painted glass by William Peckitt of York, now in the cloisters, and then the highly decorated mid 19th century Victorian glass, up to the post war period and beyond, all reflecting the fashion and age in which they were created.

This has now been brought together in this wonderful guide which will help visitors and all those with a keen interest in stained glass to look, appreciate, and understand this collection of glass. I wholeheartedly commend this guide, carefully put together by Dr Stuart Bird, and beautifully illustrated with William Finnigan's photography, to all who enter Exeter Cathedral, whether to worship and pray, or simply admire the skills and craftsmanship of stained glass throughout the building. All will no doubt be greatly inspired.

Revd Andrew Johnson, Master Glazier, A.M.G.P.

INTRODUCTION

'A man who looks on glass, on it may stay his eye, or if he pleaseth through it pass, and then the heavens espy.'

George Herbert (1593-1633), The Elixir. v. 3

As the 17th-century poet wrote these lines, which became a hymn, he appreciated that stained glass is a symphony between light and colour. The translucent properties of glass allow light to diffuse through the painted images, and to be reflected and refracted through glass of various thicknesses, to create a spiritual quality unlike any other medium.

Imagine a sunny spring day before Easter with Palm Sunday approaching. You enter the Cathedral for the first time by the north-west door. The organist is practising a Handel Oratorio for Easter, with a group of choristers.

The sun streams in through the upper clerestory windows, bathing in light the magnificent vault, the longest uninterrupted Gothic stone vault in the world. The white Beer stone ribs look like palm branches forming an arch. Members of the public sit in quiet contemplation before the midday prayer, a haven from the busy streets outside.

Exeter Cathedral is one of the most outstanding buildings in the West Country - a medieval gem! How long has this Cathedral welcomed pilgrims through its doors? Who had the inspiration to create such a marvellous building? These questions are answered well in the cathedral souvenir guide and other publications, but in this guide I wish to introduce you to the wonderful stained glass windows.

This book is designed to act as a guide to looking at the windows, with descriptions of each window illustrated by William Finnigan's images, unless indicated otherwise.

The tour starts at the Great East Window which contains the best collection of medieval glass in Devon. It has undergone many changes since its installation at the beginning of the 14th century. Iconoclasm during the Reformation and the English Civil War resulted in the damage and loss of much medieval glass throughout the cathedral.

Later, many fragments of damaged medieval glass were recycled by glaziers to create windows throughout the building with lozenge shaped patterns. Examples can be found in the north window of St Edmund's Chapel, and in the ground floor windows of the south-east cloister building.

In the 18th century Dean Jeremiah Milles invited William Peckitt of York to design new glass for the Great West Window. Peckitt was the foremost glazier in this country at the time, whose glazing technique was unusual, using enamel paint rather than stained glass. Unfortunately, just over a century later the colours had deteriorated and his window was controversially removed. Some of Peckitt's glass was later re-set in the south-east cloister windows.

By the 19th century, the medieval methods of stained glass production had been rediscovered, and a major glazing programme was undertaken in the Cathedral. Most, if not all, of these new windows were memorials for individuals or organisations. At the same time the windows containing medieval glass were restored and repaired by Frederick Drake of Exeter who was employed as the cathedral's glazier.

Fortunately during WWII the important medieval glass was saved by removing it to safe storage. However the Exeter Blitz destroyed or badly damaged most of the windows remaining which were mainly of Victorian origin. During the post-war period the windows which survived in the south nave aisle were repaired, historic panels were purchased for installation in several chapels, and new windows commissioned including designs by Sir Ninian Comper, Hugh Easton, Christopher Webb and Marion Grant. Four windows were designed by the artist Arthur Frederick Erridge and one by George Cooper-Abbs, both working for the Exeter firm of J Wippell & Co.

To maintain all our windows, they have been regularly inspected with ongoing maintenance and repair. The latest conservation practices employed, including the addition of isothermal glazing to protect the large areas of the most vulnerable historic glass.

INDEX

FLOOR PLAN

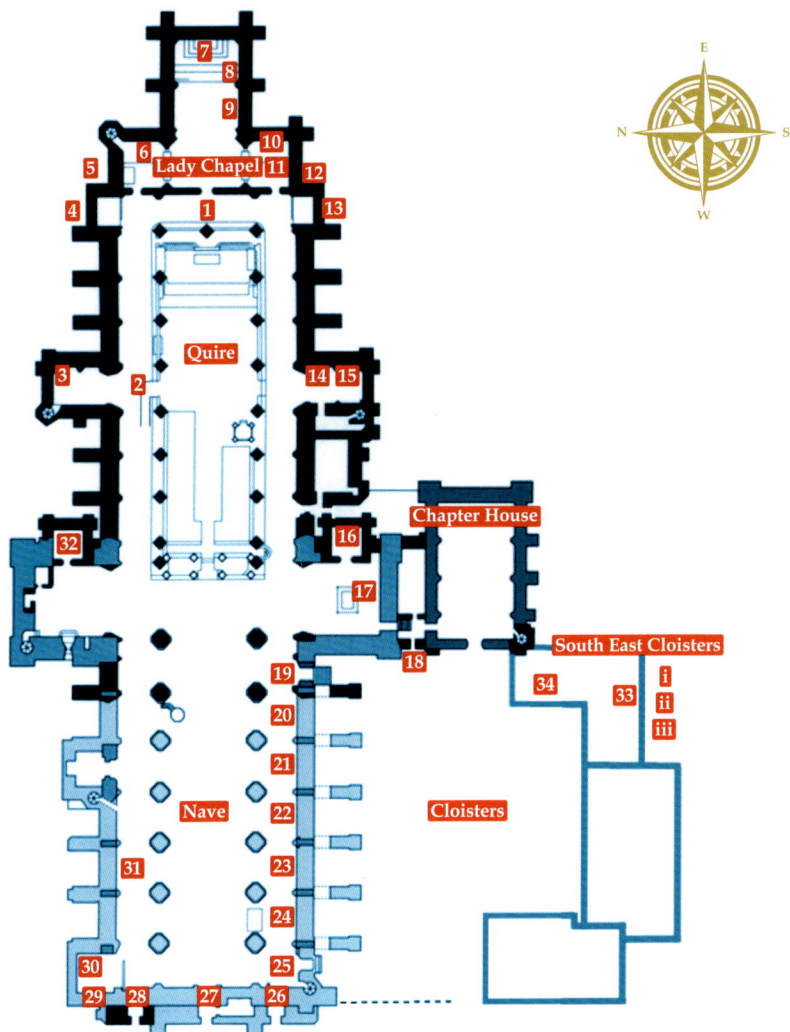

Quire

Lady Chapel

Chapter House

South East Cloisters

Nave

Cloisters

i
ii
iii

TOUR

'And God said, "Let there be light" : and there was light.'

Genesis 1 v 3.

A very warm welcome to Exeter Cathedral and this tour of the windows which begins with the Great East Window at the east end of the quire. The route then proceeds in a clockwise direction around the Cathedral with a description of each window.

1) The Great East Window

A remarkable survival at Exeter Cathedral are the Dean and Chapter's financial accounts of the Cathedral's 'fabric fund' used for building work at Exeter Cathedral between 1279 and 1514. Known as the 'fabric rolls', they were written on vellum and stored in the Cathedral Archives. Account records for the period 1279 to 1353 have been edited and translated by Audrey Erskine (1981). From this it is known that 'Master Walter the Glazier' was an artisan paid £4 10s in 1304 'for setting the glass of the high gable and 8 high windows and 6 windows in the aisles of the new Work'. The 'high windows' were in the clerestory, but the 'high gable' (summi gabuli) referred to the Great East Window itself. This is the earliest documented glass by an English glazier in England. What is so remarkable is that medieval glass in this window has survived the destruction of the Reformation, the Civil War, and WWII.

The three lights at the apex of the window are the three Prophets of the Old Testament, painted around 1300 by an unknown glazier. Now only six lights survive in this window from Master Walter, made around 1303/4. They are illustrated in the pictures attached, and you will notice the present window is in the perpendicular style. The stonework of the earlier window in the decorated style was showing signs of decay by the 1380s, and Robert Lesyngham the Master Mason from Gloucester was called upon in 1390 to redesign the Great East Window in the perpendicular style. Robert Lyen the Master Glazier was appointed to reglaze the window, retaining old glass where appropriate, and introducing new glass to his own design where necessary. In 1391 he incorporated Master Walter's glass in the new window, and painted four lights himself. These are all seen in the accompanying picture, but note the sinuous movement in St Sidwell facing St Helena. Opposite them are found two more Lyen lights depicting King Edward the Confessor facing King Edmund the Martyr holding his arrows of martyrdom. All four figures show the early use of silver stain in their crowns or hair.

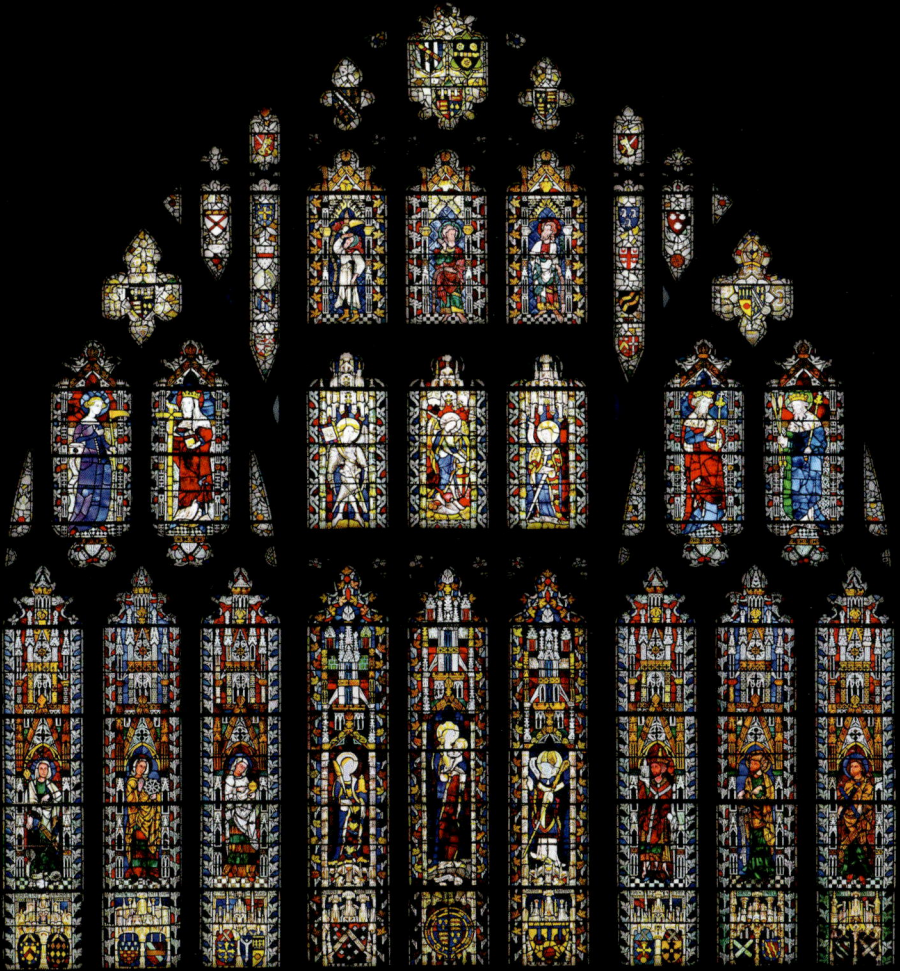

The figures in this window are : **Top tier :** Abraham; Moses; Isaiah.

Middle tier : St Sidwell; St Helena; An Archangel; Archangel Michael; St Catherine; King Edward the Confessor; King Edmund the Martyr.

Bottom Tier : St Margaret of Antioch; St Catherine; St Mary Magdalene; St Barbara; Virgin and Child; St Martin of Tours; St Peter; St Paul; St Andrew.

The three Prophets Abraham; Moses and Isaiah.
Painted by an unknown artist around 1300.

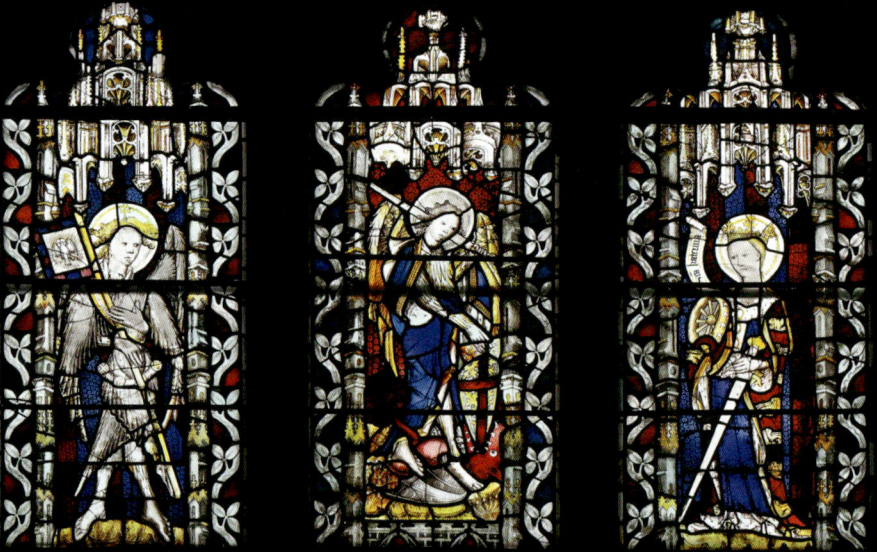

An Archangel, St Michael and St Catherine. Local atelier 15th century.

St Sidwell and St Helena by Robert Lyen 1391.

King Edward the Confessor and King Edmund by Robert Lyen 1391.

St Barbara, Virgin Mary and Child, and St Martin of Tours.
Local atelier 15th century.

St Margaret of Antioch, St Catherine and St Mary Magdalene. Artist - Master Walter the Glazier. 1303/4.

St Peter, St Paul and St Andrew. Artist : Master Walter the Glazier. 1303/4.

After the iconoclasm of the Reformation, the window lost its central lights. These were replaced by medieval glass from the Chapter House by Joseph Tucker in the 1750s. These figures have been attributed to a local atelier and were painted in a similar style to the figures found at St Michael's Church, Doddiscombsleigh. Between 1884 and 1896 more work was carried out by the Cathedral glazier Frederick Drake (1838-1920), including a remodelling of the Virgin and Child to make this figure taller than the flanking saints. The medieval glass was removed in September 1939 and taken to safety to Sydenham House, near Tavistock. The window has gone through many refurbishments summarized by the image below, showing the surviving medieval glass according to the research by John Allan the Exeter Cathedral Archaeologist, compared to the window as it looks today. These changes are well described in the excellent book written by Chris Brooks and David Evans in 1989 on the Great East Window. The clarity of the glass has recently been improved in the Great East Window, as it was cleaned in 2018, and is now protected by isothermal glazing provided by Chapel Studios. More is still to be discovered about this fascinating window, which John Allan has recently described wonderfully in the 2019 Annual Report of the Friends of Exeter Cathedral.

Present appearance and (right) the extent of the surviving medieval glass.
Artist : Master Walter the Glazier. 1303/4. (Interpretation courtesy of John Allan.)

Surviving medieval glass

Walter the Glazier 1301–4

Robert Lyen 1391

Unknown C15th

Transferred by Tucker from Cathedral, 1751–2

Transferred by Tucker from Chapter House, 1751–2

Peckitt/Godfrey, 1765–70

Drake, 1884–96

Roseveare 1948

Chapel Studio 1984–6

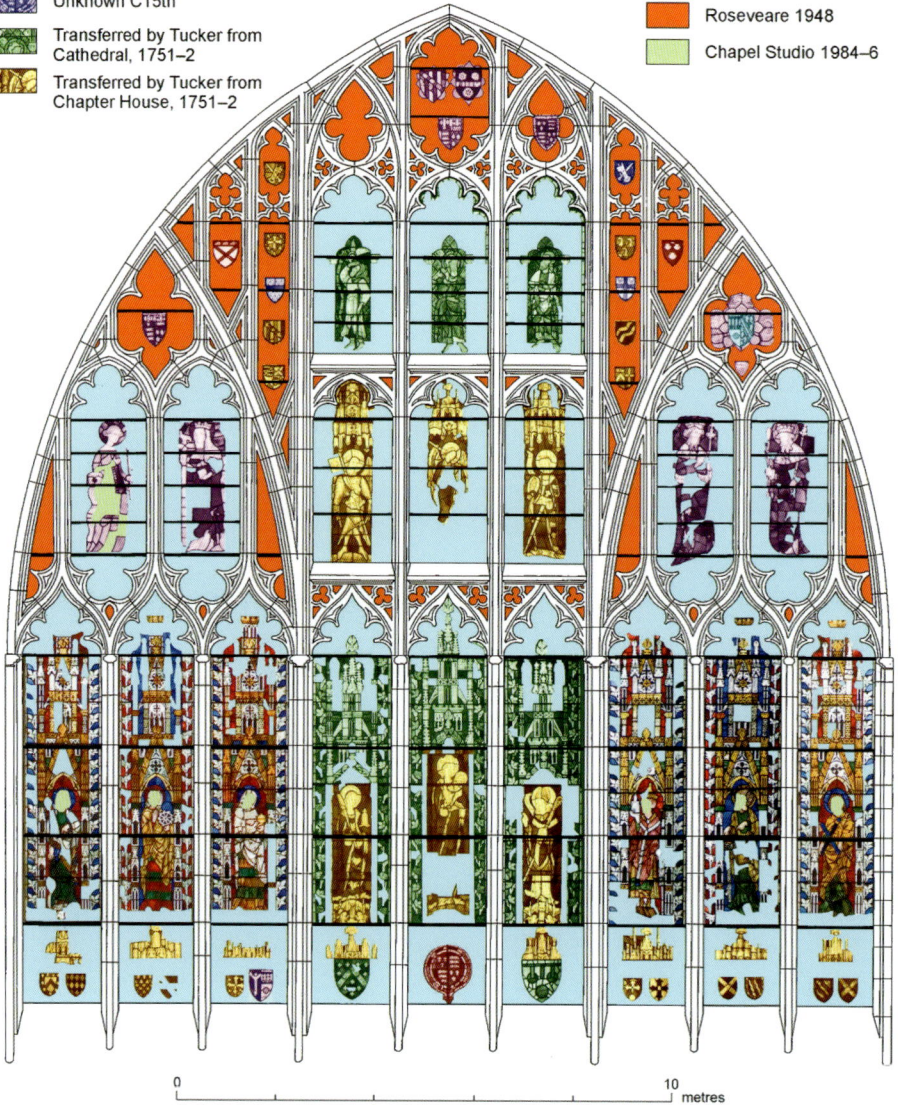

0   10 metres

Interpretation of the window in 2018. Medieval glass is shown in colour, tinted according to the phase represented, post-medieval glass shown as colour blocks. (Interpretation courtesy of John Allan).

2) North Presbytery Window

This can be found high up in the clerestory nearly opposite the Bishop's Throne. Brooks and Evans noted this window is the only survivor of the clerestory windows installed by Master Walter the Glazier in 1303. What is surprising is that it survives with most of its original glass, medieval leading, and ferramenta. This four light decorated style window contains the figures of four Apostles under decorated canopies, and set in grisaille glass. They are (from left to right) the Saints Philip the Apostle, James the Great, Matthew and Thomas. It is thought that their faces were removed during Bishop Joseph Hall's episcopacy (1621-41) to save them from Puritanical iconoclasm. In 1947, Lyon John Rosevear (1887-1971) re-installed the medieval figures and restored the tracery lights containing a medley of glass, some pieces of which were signed by the earlier glaziers. This window like the Great East Window is now protected by isothermal glazing.

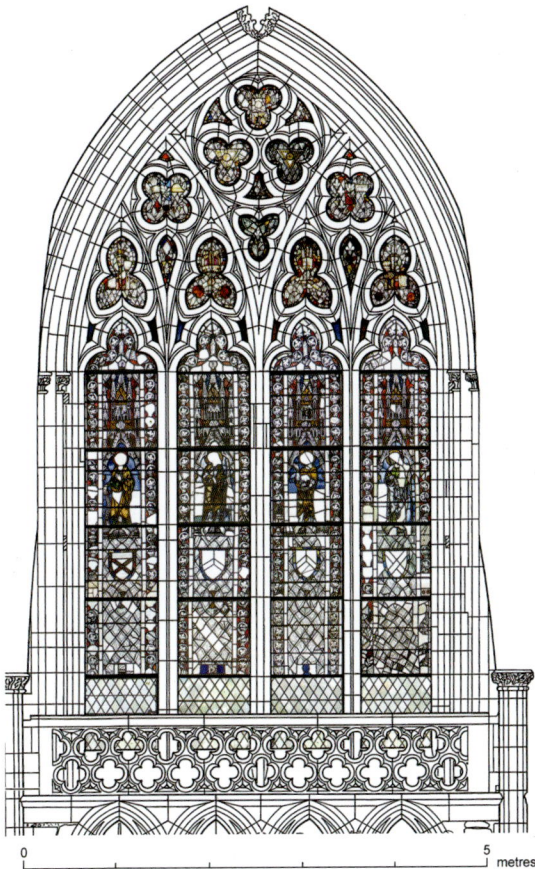

3) Chapel of St Andrew and St Catherine

The East window of the north bay commemorates the loss of
life of the officers and men on board HMS Exeter in the Java
Sea in 1942, and those who died in captivity. All three lights
are treated as one window by the famous Scottish architect,
Sir Ninian Comper (1864-1960), depicting a young beardless
Christ calming the storm on the Sea of Galilee and walking on
water apparently away from the boat, with St Peter in the left
hand light. Note Sir Ninian Comper's characteristic features:
his use of vibrant blue colours, and strawberry motif, in the
right hand bottom corner of the window. The donors were the survivors, their families,
and the families of those who were lost. As part of their annual reunion, members of the
HMS Exeter Association gather here for a commemoration service.

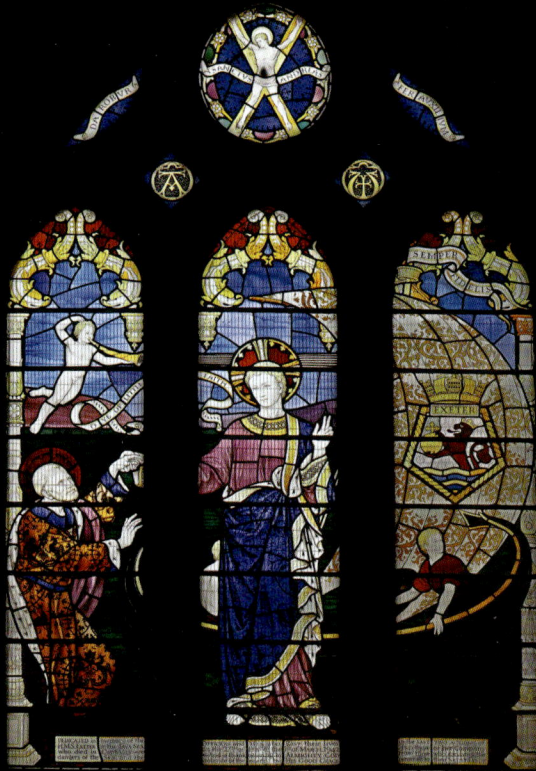

HMS Exeter Memorial Window, signed by the artist : Sir Ninian Comper.

4 & 5) Speke Chantry Chapel

Sir John Speke (1442-1518) was an MP and Sheriff of Devon. His chantry chapel mirrors in style the Oldham Chantry Chapel, which is described later.

Both windows in the Speke Chantry Chapel were reglazed during the post-war period. In the 1870s the North window had glass provided by Clayton & Bell as a memorial to Archdeacon Bartholomew. This was lost in 1942.

4) The North window now has roundels and shields with heraldic glass set in plain glass quarries. Some may have originated from the Great East Window in the 1391 refurbishment.

Speke Chantry Chapel north window.

Angel with Harp (c.1340).

5) The East window has just one roundel with a beautiful angel playing a harp and made of pot metal glass with silver-staining in the angel's hair.. The style is similar to that of the Virgin Mary and Child in the Great East Window at Wells Cathedral dated c1340,

6) Chapel of St John the Evangelist

The East window is composed of five lights glazed and inserted there after WWII. It is constructed on a grisaille background with heraldic motifs (with no links to the Carew family whose monument is situated here), and the image of three donor canons. The canons are thought to have originated from the East window of the Chapter House, having been found before 1920 in a box of glass in the Grandisson Chapel, situated next to the Great West Door.

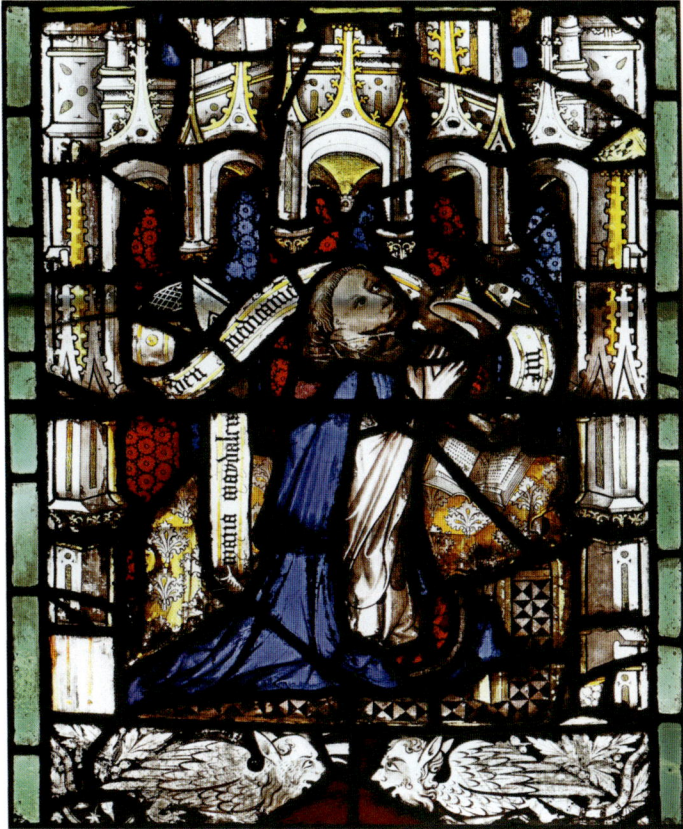

Detail of Donor Canon in the east window of the Chapel of St John the Evangelist.

7, 8 & 9) Lady Chapel

The east window initially had medieval glass, but some of it was moved to the Great East Window in 1751 during the refurbishment under Charles Lyttelton (Dean of Exeter 1748-62) and Jeremiah Milles (Dean of Exeter 1762-84), both antiquarians. Later under the restoration of Sir George Gilbert Scott (1811-78), new glass by Clayton & Bell was installed in the five Lady Chapel windows. The east window was a gift of Edward Charles Harington (Chancellor of Exeter 1847-81) in memory of his sister. The four north and south windows were dedicated to the memory of Henry Phillpotts (Bishop of Exeter 1830-69). These windows were lost in 1942.

7) Dorothy Marion Grant (1912-88) was commissioned to provide the present east window in 1951. The subject 'Triumph of Right over Wrong' is depicted through a collection of scenes, most of which relate to the Blessed Virgin Mary, the dedication of this chapel. The central scene is of Mary with the infant Christ surrounded by figures of the nativity, together with (on the left) Eve tempting Adam and the Archangel Gabriel announcing to Mary that she will give birth to Christ, and (on the right) Mary with St John at Christ's Crucifixion and Mary glorified in Heaven. Marion signed the window, and it was unveiled in the Coronation year.

Mary with the infant Christ

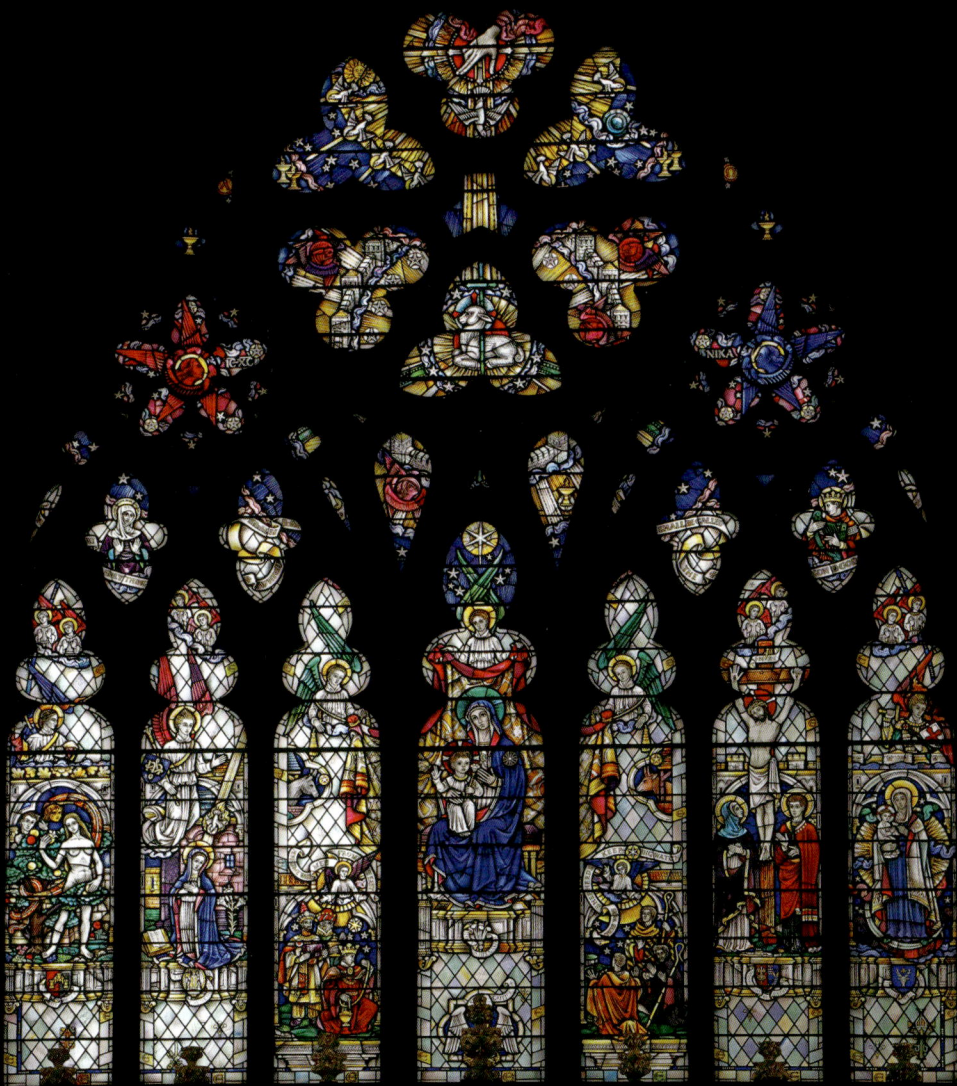

Lady Chapel E window by Marion Grant

8) The pair of windows on the north side were reglazed with plain glass quarries and a new east window was commissioned in 1951. Whilst in 1955 panels of the Costessey Collection were purchased and installed on the south side. These panels, which are mainly 16th-century Flemish glass depicting biblical scenes, were inserted into plain glass quarries.

The left hand window on the south side contains panels depicting Old Testament scenes. The upper panels (left to right) are: Tubal-Cain the first artificer in metals (Genesis 4); Moses during the battle with the Amalekites (Exodus 17); Samson removing the gates of Gaza (Judges 16). The lower panels (left to right) are: ; Joab slaying Amasa (2 Samuel 20); Elisha and the mocking children (2 Kings 2); Elisha raising the child of the Shunammite woman (2 Kings 4).

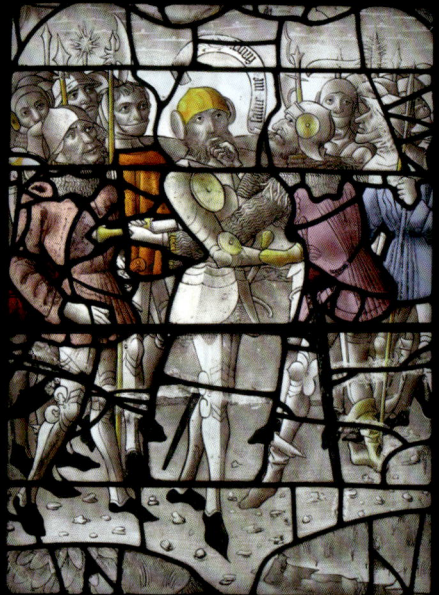

Costessey Collection Old Testament panels.

The image of Samson with the gates of Gaza comes from a Flemish block book c1465. It was called the Biblia Pauperum or Poor Man's Bible, and was clearly part of a type-antitype series. The Old Testament event (the type) prefigures an event in the Gospel (the antitype). The image of Samson removing the gates of Gaza symbolises the Resurrection of Christ because, like Samson, he rose in the middle of the night and cheated death. The gates of Gaza symbolise the gates of Hell, which Christ conquered by rising from the dead.

Samson with the
gates of Gaza.

Samson with the gates of Gaza from a Flemish block book
©Victoria and Albert Museum, London.

9) The right hand window on the south side contains panels from the New Testament. From left to right these are Judas being bribed to betray Christ; St Anne with her daughter, the Blessed Virgin and the infant Christ; and finally a French panel depicting doubting Thomas.

Judas being bribed to betray Christ. Rarely depicted in stained glass.

St Anne with her daughter, the Blessed Virgin
and the infant Christ

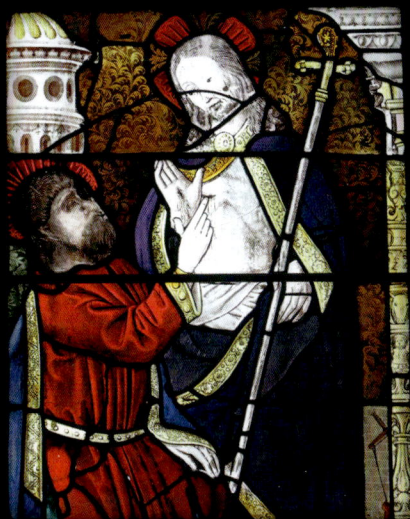

Doubting Thomas

10 & 11) Chapel of St Gabriel

10) The East window contains some medieval panels inserted after WWII, and the most interesting being the fine central panel of the Crucifixion which was purchased in 1949 for £150. The source is unknown, but stylistically it's similar to the central figures in the Great East Window, and the images of the donor canons in the Chapel of St John the Evangelist, who are thought by Brooks and Evans to have been painted by the same master, and to have originated from the same local atelier. A detailed account of the Crucifixion panel is provided by John Allan in the 2021 Annual Report of the Friends of Exeter Cathedral.

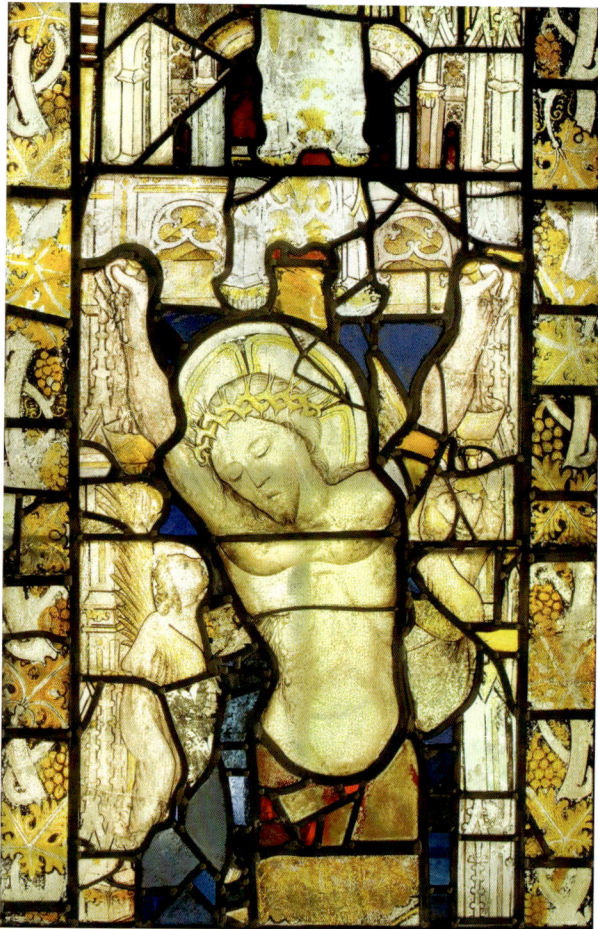

Crucifixion Panel (image by Gary Young after the panel was refurbished by Holy Well Glass in 2021).

11) The South window contains some of the finest grisaille glass in the Cathedral, and probably designed for this chapel in c1300 on its completion. It was saved from destruction in WWII, having been restored by Frederick Drake in 1877 under Scott's refurbishment, and then reinserted in 1951 by Lyon John Rosevear. The grisaille glass contains wonderfully delicate tendrils, painted on very white glass imported from Rouen in France. Recent X-ray fluorescence analysis by David Dungworth on this window, suggests much of the original glass had been so well restored by Drake, it is indistinguishable from the original.

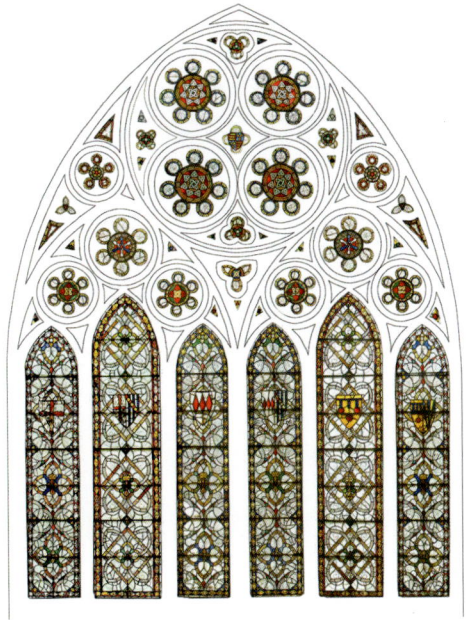

South Window of St Gabriel's Chapel (picture by Gary Young after Holy Well Glass refurbished it in 2021).

An engraving by Frederick Drake in 1877 after he restored the South Window of St Gabriel's Chapel. Note that some of the heraldic elements were moved after WWII.

12 & 13) Oldham Chantry Chapel

Hugh Oldham (Bishop of Exeter 1505-19) and Sir John Speke were good friends, and the Oldham Chapel has some similarities to the Speke Chapel described previously. There are two windows, both of which were reglazed after WWII.

12) The East window has some medieval fragments set in plain glass quarries. One roundel is striking and depicts an archangel's head, with silver stained hair, halo, and a diadem-cross. There are other similar examples of archangels set in medieval glass; for example there is a depiction of an archangel in the Great East Window of the Cathedral, and at St Michael's Church in Doddiscombsleigh, there is a window showing Archangel Michael, probably painted in the late 15th century, in the International Gothic style by the same locally based master, according to Brooks and Evans.

Archangel roundel in the east window of
the Oldham Chantry Chapel.

The east window of the Oldham Chantry Chapel.

13) The South window of five lights contains some medieval grisaille glass, originally from Salisbury Cathedral. It was donated by Dr Baker, a former pupil of Manchester Grammar School, and the 'alumnus' mentioned in the inscription of five lines in Roman capitals: 'In piam ac Gratum memoriam Hugouis Oldham fundatoris alumnus scholae Mancuniensis dedicavit.' This can be translated as 'In grateful memory to Hugh Oldham from the former pupils of Manchester Grammar, the school which he founded.'

The south window of the Oldham Chantry Chapel.

14 & 15) Chapel of St James

The medieval chapel of St James was destroyed by a direct hit from a high explosive bomb dropped by the Luftwaffe on the night of May 4th 1942, Fortunately there was no loss of life in the Cathedral.

The rebuilt chapel is similar to the medieval chapel of St Andrew and St Catherine, its counterpart on the north side of the Cathedral, but has no south window. Both chapels have two eastern windows with plain tracery and three lights.

14) The left hand window was designed in 1976 by Frederick W Cole (1908-98) from the Canterbury Stained Glass Studio. It is a memorial to the Devonshire and Dorset Regiment, with a figure of St Alban who was a Roman soldier, martyred after sheltering a Christian priest, and subsequently converted to Christianity. St Alban is flanked by the armorial bearings of the Devon and Dorset County Councils, and the head tracery shows the Devonshire and Dorset Regimental badge.

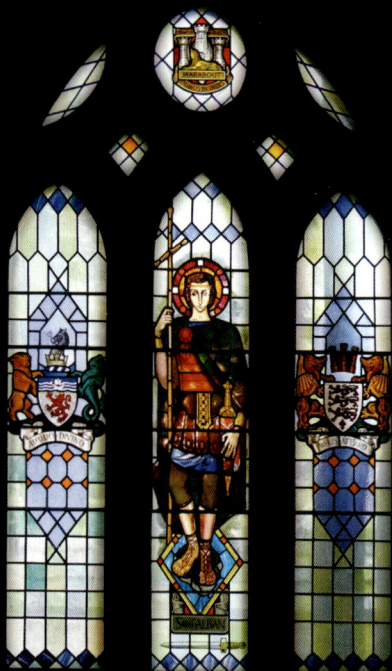

Figure of St Alban who was a Roman soldier designed by Frederick Cole in 1976. (Image kindly supplied by Rex Harris).

15) The window to the right depicts St George, England's patron Saint, slaying the Dragon, in a dramatic pose which covers all three lights. The glazier in 1959 was Hugh Easton (1906-65), who also designed the Battle of Britain memorial window filling the east end of the RAF Chapel in Westminster Abbey. His work can be identified by his weathervane motif in the bottom right hand corner of the St George window. This window is a memorial to Hugh Fortescue, 4th Earl Fortescue (1854-1932), who was Lord Lieutenant of Devon (1904-28). The Fortescue arms, surmounted by an Earl's coronet, are in the upper light

St George and the Dragon window designed by Hugh Easton in 1959.
(Image kindly supplied by Janice Lane).
The image to the right is Hugh Easton's signature - image by the author

16) Chapel of St John the Baptist

This chapel, off the south transept, features an East window with tracery and four lights, depicting scenes from the life of St John the Baptist. The local artist was Arthur Frederick Erridge (1899-1961) of J Wippell & Co, the clerical outfitters, and church furnishings company established in Exeter for more than 200 years. The window was installed in 1961, replacing an earlier window by Clayton & Bell installed in c.1870, but lost in 1942. It commemorated the Barnes and Heberden families. Ralph Barnes (d.1820) was residentiary Canon at the Cathedral from 1769, becoming Archdeacon of Totnes, then Chancellor of the Cathedral. William Heberden (1710-1801) was a well-known Physician and his son Thomas Heberden (1754-1843) was a Canon of Exeter Cathedral.

ARTHUR·F·ERRIDGE
DESIGNER

You can see the designer's name clearly in the bottom right hand corner. Arthur Erridge worked for J. Wippell & Co., and the 'W' of Wippell is superimposed on the sheep shearer's hook. Not surprisingly the family were sheep farmers.

St John the Baptist window, commemorating the Barnes and Heberden families.

17) South Transept

Only the tracery lights remain in this large six light window, commemorating Sir John Taylor Coleridge (1790-1876), an English Judge, and nephew to Samuel Taylor Coleridge (1772-1834) the poet. The Coleridge family home is Ottery St Mary, hence the otter in the tracery light and family crest. (The Martyrs' Pulpit in the Cathedral nave commemorates Bishop John Coleridge Patteson, nephew to Sir John). The window was installed during Sir George Gilbert Scott's restoration and executed by Clayton & Bell, the lower lights being lost during 1942.

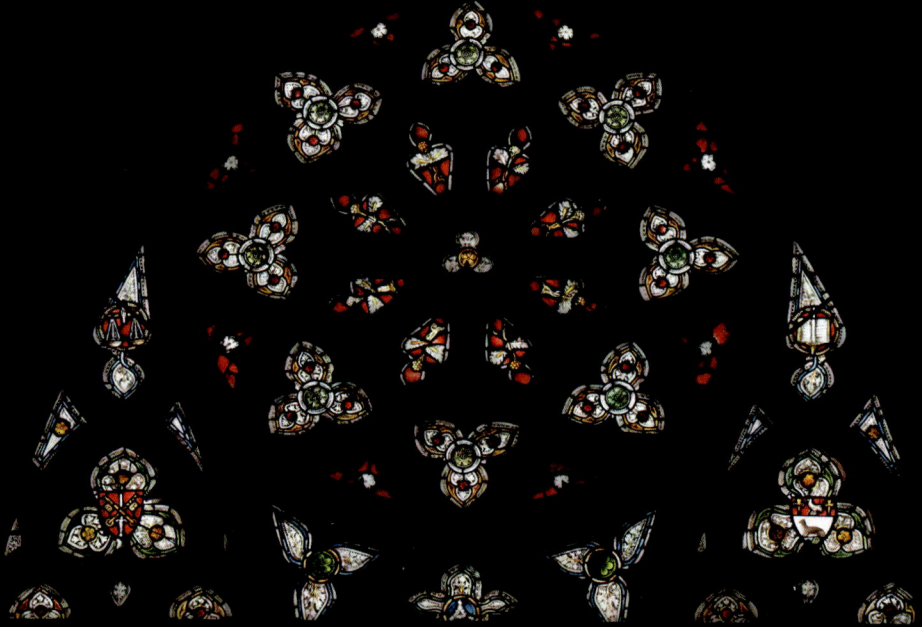

South Transept tracery in a window commemorating Sir John Taylor Coleridge designed by Clayton & Bell.

Close-up of the Otter shield, the family crest of the Coleridge family of Ottery St Mary. Courtesy of John Allan.

18) The Drake Memorial Window

This three-light window without tracery is located above the door opposite the former Chapel of the Holy Ghost. It was installed in 1921 to commemorate Frederick Drake (1838-1920), an expert in stained glass and Cathedral glazier for 40 years, and William Bellringer, the supervisor of Drake's glazing business. Frederick Drake is depicted in the guise of the Blessed James of Ulm (a 15th-century Dominican monk from Germany), the patron of Glaziers, with armorial bearings in the roundel above. He is holding up a vidimus for the Exeter Cathedral window commemorating Bishop Grandisson which Frederick Drake designed during the 1880s. (See also window 26 and the 2019 Annual Report of the Friends of Exeter Cathedral). This is an unusual, if not unique example, of an ecclesiastical glazier being commemorated in glass by his son Frederick Morris Drake (also known as Maurice), who, on his father's retirement, followed him as Cathedral glazier. When the window was restored by Daphne Drake (1901-92) after WWII, she added the dedications to her father Frederick Morris Drake (1875-1923) and his brother Wilfred (1879-1948) both 'distinguished glaziers of this city'. Three generations of the Drake family were Exeter Cathedral glaziers, starting with Frederick in 1880 and ending with Daphne whose last work in the Cathedral was the restoration of the Drake Memorial Window.
What a great legacy one family gave to our nation and Exeter Cathedral!

Close-up from the Drake Memorial window of the vidimus of the Grandisson window.

The Drake Memorial Window.

19) The Courtenay Bishops Window

The Courtenay family have had a long association with Exeter Cathedral. The Earls of Devon family seat is Powderham Castle on the west bank of the River Exe a few miles south of Exeter.

This short window with four lights in the South Aisle above Bishop Brewer's doorway commemorates the Courtenay Bishops, two of whom were Bishops of Exeter. This replaces the previous window of 1877, damaged beyond repair during WWII, and was painted by AF Erridge (of J Wippell & Co.) in 1955. The Bishops commemorated are William, Richard, Peter and Henry named at the base of each light, and identified by their attributes or heraldic achievements. William Courtenay (1342-96) was made prebendary of Exeter, Wells and York, before being consecrated Bishop of Hereford in 1370. He was translated to the see of London in 1375, and became Archbishop of Canterbury in 1381. Richard Courtenay (d.1415) was nephew to William, and became Dean of Wells, before being consecrated Bishop of Norwich in 1413. Peter Courtenay (1432-92) was great-nephew of Bishop Richard Courtenay. He was consecrated Bishop of Exeter in 1478 and gave the Cathedral the large 'Peter' bell which hangs in the north tower. In 1487 he was promoted to the see of Winchester where he died in 1492. Henry Reginald Courtenay (1741-1803) was nominated Bishop of Bristol in 1794, and translated to the see of Exeter where he served from 1797 until his death in 1803.

The Courtenay Bishops Window

20) The Cathedral Builders Window

The lower panels of this window contain the coats of arms and names of nine people who contributed in different ways to the construction and enhancement of the buildings used as Exeter Cathedral. They are : King Athelstan and Bishops Warelwast, Bronescombe, Quivil, Bytton, Stapledon, Grandisson, Brantyngham and Lacy. The window was created and signed in 1955 by George Cooper-Abbs (1901-66) the senior designer of J Wippell & Co. It replaced an earlier window by Frederick Drake (1889) commemorating Thomas Latimer, a reforming journalist and editor of the Western Times, which was destroyed in 1942. This window depicts Christ in Glory, flanked by the four Latin Doctors of the early Christian Church. They are named and can also be recognised by their attributes, namely the lion at the feet of St Jerome, the dove by the ear of St Gregory, the scourge and beehive of St Ambrose and the black habit of the order of St Augustine of Hippo.

Above - George Cooper-Abbs signature found in the bottom right hand panel. Pictured by the author.

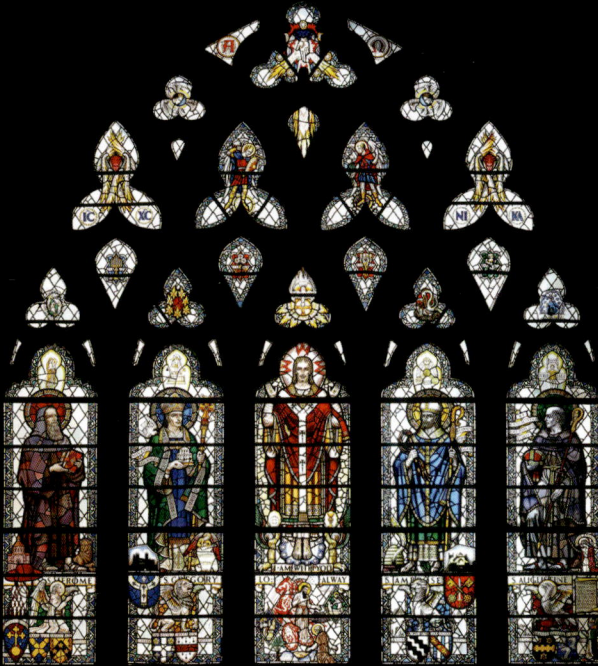

The Cathedral Builders Window

21) The Charles Arthur Turner Window

This commemorative window by James Powell & Sons, was damaged in 1942, and later restored by Powell & Sons (Whitefriars) Ltd., of London. It epitomises Turner's life of Justice in the tracery lights, and depicts Moses flanked on the left by Samuel and David, and on the right by Nehemiah and Amos. The wall plaque below records that the window commemorates Charles Turner's life as a Judge and Secretary General of India.

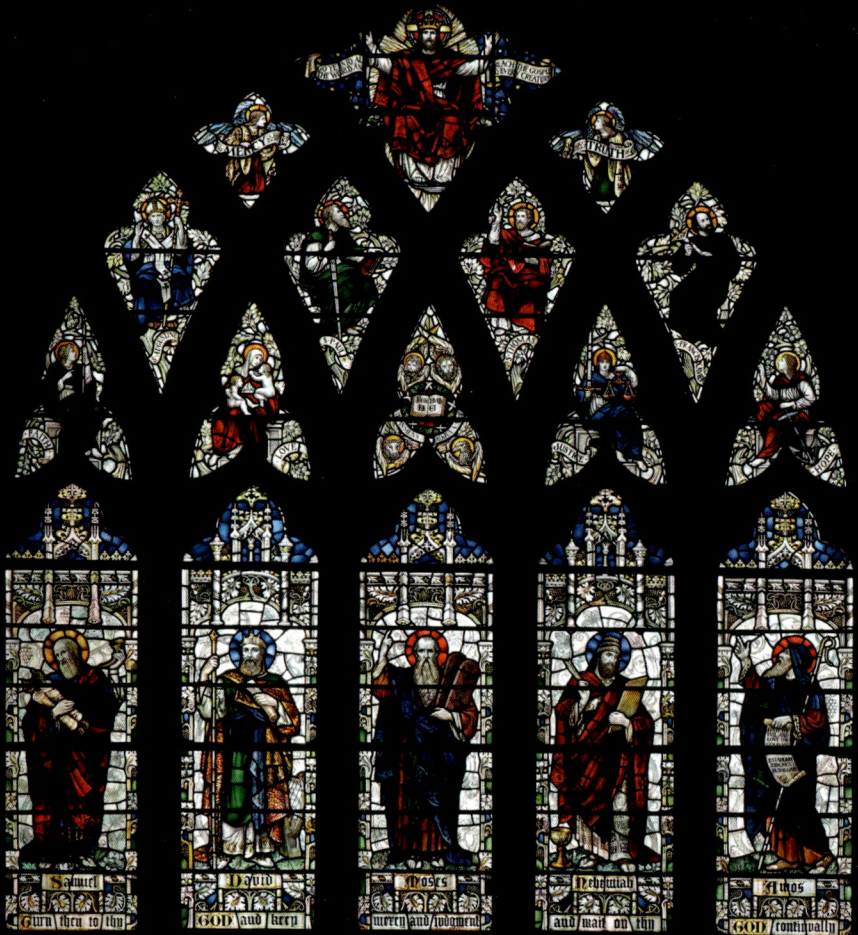

The Charles Arthur Turner Memorial Window

22) The South African War Memorial Window

This window commemorates Devonians who lost their lives in the South African Wars (1899-1902), especially those in the Devonshire Regiment, the colours of which (red and green) have been worked in very effectively. Clayton & Bell, of London who were leading glaziers and responsible for the windows in Truro Cathedral, were called upon to paint this window in 1903. It was damaged in 1942, and restored by the same company. The iconography is of the Church Militant: the central figure of Christ is flanked by the figure of King Alfred and Abraham on the left, with Joshua and King Edward I on the right. When this window was installed, panels inscribed with the names of those commemorated were mounted on the wall below the window, but later moved to the north transept.

The South African War Memorial Window.

23) The WWII Air Raid of Exeter Memorial Window

Two hundred and fifty people lost their lives in Exeter during the air raids of 1942. This window commemorates the damage and restoration of the Cathedral and City of Exeter. It was paid for by Mayor Cottey's Preservation Fund of 1951. The window was created and signed in 1957 by Christopher Rahere Webb (1886-1966), one of the finest glass painters of the 20th century, who worked with Sir Ninian Comper (see window 3). Note that Webb uses the whole window, dispensing with conventional canopy work, and the groups of figures are framed by twining foliage. The central light depicts the Risen Lord with angels trumpeting in flanking lights. Below kneels St Peter in a moving pose, offering up to God the Cathedral for safekeeping, against the conflagration of the surrounding city. Bishop William Warelwast, who initiated the construction of the Romanesque cathedral, is shown on the left, with a mason and organ builder on the right, repairing the damaged Cathedral. A note of optimism is depicted in the upper lights as a full circle of ringing bells heralds peace - an unusual subject in stained glass.

The WWII Air Raid of Exeter Memorial Window, signed in the bottom right hand panel by Christopher Webb using the figure of St Christopher. On the front cover a close-up of an angel holding a shield bearing the arms of Exeter Cathedral.

A close-up from the Air Raid window depicting St. Peter with a model of
Exeter Cathedral, and asking Christ to spare it from destruction.

24) The Tanner Memorial Window

Capt. Thomas Tanner (1788-1863) was Mayor of Exeter in 1859. He and his wife Bridget, are commemorated in this window. The original window by Burlison & Grylls in 1906 was damaged in 1942, but repaired and restored. Both John Burlison (1843-91) and Thomas Grylls (1845-1913) had trained under Clayton & Bell. The window depicts a Roman Centurion in front of the three crosses on Calvary, flanked by St Thomas and St Bridget, saints whose names correspond to those of the couple commemorated. The individual figures are under canopies in the medieval style. The outer lights depict the various acts of Jesus around the Sea of Galilee. Capt. Thomas Tanner had previously been Commodore of Surat for the East India Company.

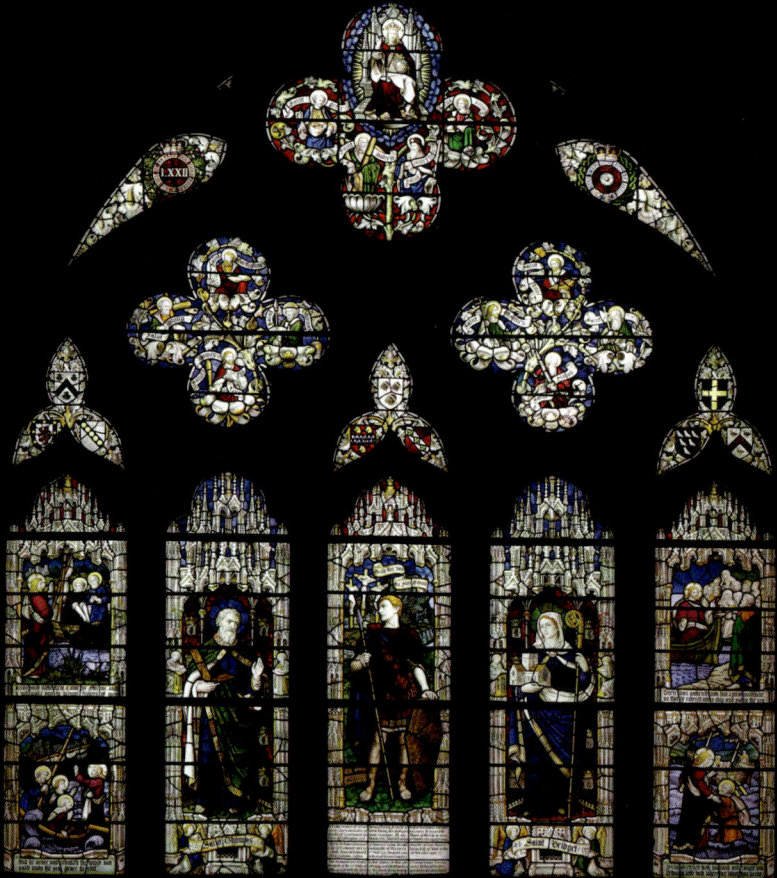

The Tanner Memorial Window.

25) The Nativity Window

This window has five lights, but shorter than others in the South Aisle, due to the doors to the cloisters and to the spiral stairs to the roof. It commemorates Edward Andrew Sanders JP (1813-1905), Mayor of Exeter in 1850/1, Deputy Lieutenant of Devon, and senior partner in the Exeter Bank. AF Erridge of J Wippell & Co painted this window and three others in the Cathedral after WWII. The colourful scene over five lights depicts the Shepherds and the Wise Men bringing their gifts to baby Jesus, and includes a procession of civil dignitaries in the upper tracery.

The Nativity Window.

26) The Grandisson Memorial Window

John Grandisson (Bishop of Exeter 1327-69) was a man of letters, of great artistic taste, who made a major contribution to Exeter Cathedral. His memorial window glazed by Frederick Drake in the 1880s (see window 18) was, sadly, destroyed in 1942. Lyon John Rosevear inserted this replica window using Drake's designs in 1949. The work was supported by contributions from the Urban District of Ottery St Mary. It is composed of Bishop Grandisson in the centre light in his Bishop's mass vestments, flanked by two kneeling donor canons holding the Cathedral and the Church of Ottery St Mary. Bishop Grandisson saw the completion of the Cathedral under his long episcopacy, and founded the collegiate church in Ottery St Mary. He was laid to rest in his chapel situated next to the Cathedral's great west door.

The Grandisson Memorial Window.

27) The Great West Window

This window has been reglazed at least three times since the Reformation. In 1764 Dean Jeremiah Milles called upon the leading glass painter of the day, William Peckitt (1731-95) of York, to provide painted glass in the Great West Window. His window, completed in 1767, no longer survives, although the tinted picture by John Tothill gives us an idea of its appearance with figures under canopies, and elaborate armorials. Some portions have been saved and appear in the south-east cloister windows (33 & 34). They are mainly armorial panels of some noble families who sponsored William Peckitt's window. By 1902 the tracery in the Great West Window was in poor repair, and the stained glass began to fade and turn yellow. William Peckitt used enamel paint on the glass, rather than the earlier techniques used by medieval glaziers, which had been lost or forgotten (See John Tothill's engraving of William Peckitt's window below).

Peckitt's window was replaced in 1904 by T.J.Grylls of Burlison & Grylls who executed and installed the new window under the direction of George Frederick Bodley (1827-1907). The new window was a memorial to Archbishop Frederick Temple (1821-1902). He was Bishop of Exeter (1869-85), subsequently Bishop of London (1885-96), and then Archbishop of Canterbury (1896-1902) until his death aged 81.

As many of the windows in the Cathedral suffered the same fate, this window was also lost in 1942. It now contains similar subject matter to the pre-war window, and was installed by Reginald Bell & MC Farrer Bell at Clayton & Bell in 1953. This window is a memorial to Archbishops Frederick Temple and his son William Temple (1881-1944), born in Exeter, who was Archbishop of Canterbury (1942-1944) until his death aged only 63.

The nine figures in the lower part of the window are from left to right : - King Athelstan, Bishop Leofric, Bishop Stapledon, King Edward the Confessor, St Peter, Queen Edytha (wife of Edward), Bishop Grandisson, Bishop Coverdale, and Archbishop Frederick Temple.

The tracery elements include representations of the Almighty, the Agnus Dei, angels, and symbols of the four Evangelists.

John Tothill's engraving - surveyor to the Chapter (1759-1800),
opposite is the present Great West Window.

The Great West Window

The Great West Window nine lights

SAINT PETER

St Peter close-up.

Tracery Lights of the Great West Window.

28) The RD Blackmore Memorial Window

Richard Dodderidge Blackmore (1825-1900) was educated at Blundell's School, Tiverton, and spent his early life in the beautiful countryside of Exmoor. This small three light window commemorates the famous Victorian author of 'Lorna Doone'. The window depicts Jonathan, King David, and Samson who are meant to represent in scriptural form the characteristics of John Ridd the hero of Lorna Doone, namely love and tenderness, courage, and strength. The tracery lights depict incidents from the novel. The original window was painted by Percy Bacon Bros of London in 1904. The subscribers included Thomas Hardy, Rudyard Kipling and JM Barrie. Following serious damage in 1942, this window was later replaced by AF Erridge in a more modern depiction of the same main characters.

RD Blackmore Memorial Window.

THIS TABLET AND THE WINDOW ABOVE ARE A
TRIBUTE OF ADMIRATION AND AFFECTION
TO THE MEMORY
OF

RICHARD DODDRIDGE BLACKMORE, M.A.

SON OF THE

REV. JOHN BLACKMORE.

EDUCATED AT BLUNDELL'S SCHOOL, TIVERTON;
AND EXETER COLLEGE, OXFORD, (SCHOLAR;)
BARRISTER OF THE MIDDLE TEMPLE, 1852;
AUTHOR OF "LORNA DOONE," "SPRINGHAVEN" AND OTHER WORKS;
BORN AT LONGWORTH, BERKS, 7 JUNE, 1825;
DIED AT TEDDINGTON, MIDDLESEX, 20 JAN.,1900.

"INSIGHT, AND HUMOUR, AND THE RHYTHMIC ROLL
OF ANTIQUE LORE, HIS FERTILE FANCIES SWAY'D,
AND WITH THEIR VARIOUS ELOQUENCE ARRAY'D
HIS STERLING ENGLISH, PURE AND CLEAN AND WHOLE."
A.J.M.

"HE ADDED CHRISTIAN COURTESY, AND THE HUMILITY
OF ALL THOUGHTFUL MINDS, TO A CERTAIN GRAND
AND GLORIOUS GIFT OF RADIATING HUMANITY."
Cradock Nowell.

RD Blackmore memorial tablet by the NW door is by Harry Hems of Exeter.

29 & 30) Chapel of St Edmund

29) The west window is a memorial to those men of the Devonshire Regiment who lost their lives in the various conflicts fought by the Regiment. It is an Early English style window with two lights, with a small lozenge at the apex containing the badge of the Devonshire Regiment. The artist Reginald Otto Bell, of Clayton & Bell 'signed' the window in 1948 (in the bottom right hand corner). The window depicts on the left St Michael clad in armour standing on a dragon and the right St George and the Dragon with the regimental colours, and battle honours of the Devonshire Regiment below. The window was donated by the Regiment to replace a 19th-century window destroyed in 1942 like most of the Victorian glass in the Cathedral.

Reginald Otto Bell's signature.

The Chapel of St Edmund - Devonshire Regiment Memorial Window.

30) The north window has plain glass with lozenge patterns, made from medieval glass, similar to many of the windows in Exeter Cathedral before 1942, and can still be found in the windows of the south-east cloister building (34).

31) The Devon Boroughs Window

The only stained glass in the North Nave Aisle are the Arms of ten Devon Boroughs : Great Torrington, Dartmouth, Tavistock, Barnstable, Totnes, Bideford, Plymouth, Paignton, Ilfracombe, and Torquay by Lyon John Rosevear: These boroughs were included as they contributed to the post-war restoration appeal, and the window was dedicated in 1952.

The Devon Boroughs Window.

32) Chapel of St Paul

This Chapel can be found in the north transept.

The East window with four lights contains some old glass that was returned to the Dean and Chapter in 1921 from the Architectural Association. It was used initially in the Drake Memorial Window, but after WWII it was transferred to this window. It contains starbursts in blue and gold, plus some heraldic shields belonging to among others Bishops Grandisson and Lacy, surrounded by borders of medieval fragments.

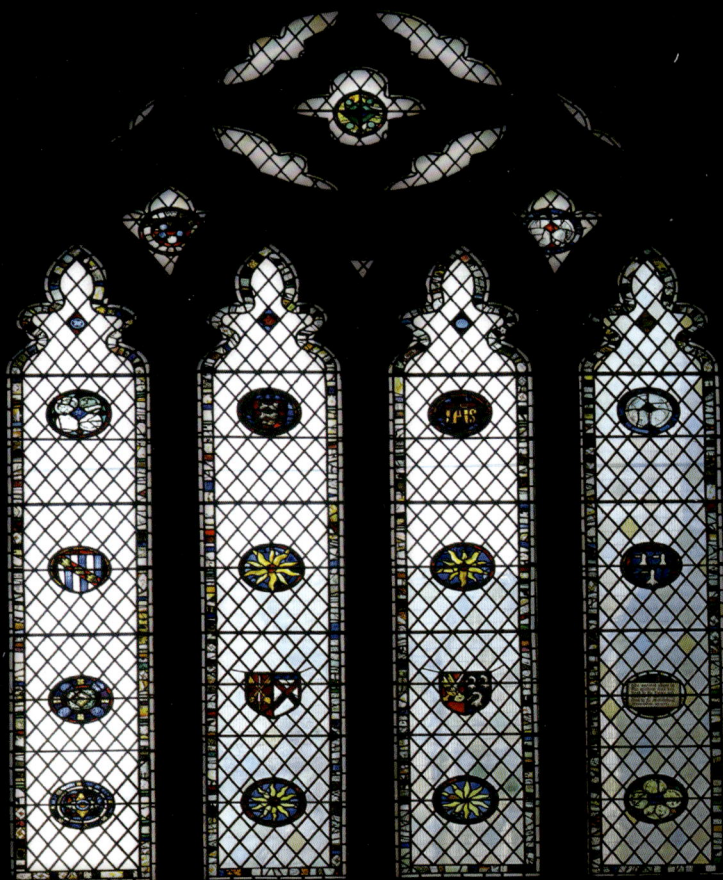

Chapel of St Paul - east window.

33 & 34) Ground Floor of the South-East Cloister Building

Two sets of windows containing re-used painted and stained glass can be found in the ground floor of the south-east cloister building.

33(i)) In the three windows facing south is a collection of 18th-century heraldic glass from William Peckitt's Great West Window. The shields are of the sponsors of Peckitt's window which was removed in 1904 as the enamel paint had badly faded. They were leaded into place in 1922 by Maurice Drake whose life was cut short in 1923, leaving the completion of the windows to his daughter Daphne.

East window in the south wall containing heraldic shields by William Peckitt.

Labels on stained glass window:

EARL OF ORFORD — DUKE OF BOLTON — DUKE OF BEDFORD — Sᴿ RIC BAMPFYLDE

Sᴿ FRANCIS DRAKE — Sᴿ STAFFORD NORTHCOTE — Sᴿ JOHN DAVIE — Sᴿ JOHN SᵀAUBYN

This central window photo was provided courtesy of Paul Scott of Flickr.

SR STAFFORD NORTHCOTE

SR JOHN DAVIE

BP GRANDISON

SR FRANCIS DRAKE

Close-ups of some heraldic shields by William Peckitt.

33(iii)) Window truncated by the adjoining cloister room. Note the inscription..

VISCOUNT COURTENAY

SEE OF EXETER

THE STAINED GLASS IN
THIS AND THE ADJOIN-
ING WINDOWS WAS
REMOVED FROM THE
GREAT WEST WINDOW
OF EXETER CATHEDRAL
1904 AND FIXED HERE
1922. IT WAS PAINTED
1766 BY WILLIAM PECK-
ITT OF YORK. BORN 1731
DIED 1795.

KINGDOM OF WESSEX

K. EDWARD THE CONFESSOR

34)) The windows in the north and west walls are quite different. The lights contain lozenge-shaped patterns made from old glass, similar to the north window in St Edmund's Chapel, and once found in many windows throughout the Cathedral. The heads of the lights and the tracery contain fragments of Peckitt's glass from his west window.

The Latin inscription at the bottom of the north window in the west wall translates to: 'In order to preserve from complete destruction the splendid work of William Peckitt of York, which were formerly displayed in the Great West Window of this church, these remains of his work, with the addition of some fragments of early glass from the church, were put back in these seven windows of the cloister under the direction of John Frederick Chanter, MA, Fellow of the Society of Antiquaries, Prebendary of this church. AD 1923'.

North window in the west wall with lozenge shaped patterns and an inscription.

In conclusion, we have seen that Exeter Cathedral has some beautiful medieval windows dating from the early 14th century, the best example being the Great East Window, the finest medieval window in Devon. In the Lady Chapel the Costessey panels are late medieval created by Flemish and French glaziers. The Georgian period is represented by the Peckitt glass in the south-east cloister room. Most of the Victorian glass was a casualty of the 1942 air raid. Some of this has been replaced, especially in the South Aisle, with a high standard of workmanship. My favourite is Mayor Cottey's appeal window commemorating the loss of life and property in the city, and the renewal thereafter. I hope you have enjoyed your journey around Exeter Cathedral, and have come to appreciate this amazing building and its beautiful windows.

BIBLIOGRAPHY

*Allan, John. 'The Great East Window.' Friends of Exeter Cathedral, Annual Report, (2019), pp. 20-27.

*Allan, John. 'Building Recording in the Clerestory of the Quire and Presbytery: Part 1, The North Side of Bay 8 and its Glass.' Friends of Exeter Cathedral, Annual Report, (2018), pp. 24-28.

*Allan, John. 'The Crucifixion Panel in St Gabriel's Chapel.' Friends of Exeter Cathedral, Annual Report, (2021), pp. 21-23.

xAtkinson, C.S. 'William Peckitt's Great West Window at Exeter Cathedral.' MPhil Thesis, (2011), University of Plymouth. (Found online at : http://hdl.handle.net/10026.i/887)

*Bird, Stuart. 'The Drake and Grandisson Memorial Windows.' Friends of Exeter Cathedral, Annual Report, (2019), pp. 33-37.

+Brooks, Chris, and Evans, David. The Great East Window of Exeter Cathedral: a glazing history, (Exeter, 1988).

+Cherry, Bridget, and Pevsner, Nikolaus. Devon - The Buildings of England. (Yale, 1991).

**Drake, Daphne. 'Frederick Drake (Glass-Painter of Exeter).' Journal of the British Society of Master Glass-Painters. (Apr 1930). Vol III, No.3, pp.105-107.

**Drake, Frederick. 'The ancient stained glass of Exeter Cathedral,' Transactions of the Exeter Diocesan Architectural Society, (Oct 2 1879), Vol IV, pp.321-327, plate XVIII.

+Drake, Maurice and Wilfred. 'Saints and their emblems'. T. Werner Laurie Ltd., London, 1916. (Free online at : archive.org/details/cu31924030663052).

=Dungworth, David. 'Exeter Cathedral: pXRF Analysis of Stained Glass,' Heritage Science Solutions, (2019). (**Note this can be consulted in the Cathedral Archive).

+Erskine, Audrey. 'The Accounts of the Fabric of Exeter Cathedral (1279-1353),' Devon and Cornwall Record Society, Part 1: 1279-1326 (Torquay), 1981 p. 35.

=Exeter Cathedral Gazetteer. (Jul 2016). Keystone Historic Building Consultants.

=Hope, The Rev Vyvyan. 'Notes on Exeter Cathedral stained glass windows,' (1957).

+Hope, V., Lloyd, J., and Erskine, Audrey M. Exeter Cathedral: a short history and description, 2nd ed. (Exeter, 1988).

xStephenson, Jane (later Cole). 'Maurice Drake, Glass Painter and the Drake Workshop, Exeter (1906-1923),' A dissertation, (Manchester, 1981).

xVidimus. 'St Edward the Confessor - Robert Lyen's work at Exeter Cathedral,' (Nov 2010). Issue 45. Centre of medieval studies, The University of York. (Free online at : www.vidimus.org/?s=Robert+Lyen)

(Note * The Annual Reports of the Friends of Exeter Cathedral are freely delivered to members. Copies can be consulted in the Library Archives.

**Journals, x Other Sources, + Books and = Unpublished Sources).

GLOSSARY

Atelier : Historically a workshop or studio used by an artist or designer.

Attribute : An object (usually symbolic) used to identify a Saint or person in art.

Block book : A short book printed from woodcuts from the 15th century to illustrate religious or secular themes.

Biblia Pauperum : Or Paupers' Bible was not intended to be bought by the poor, but used by clergy to instruct those who could not read. The name Biblia Pauperum has been given to books which tell the story of the redemption of man by Christ, set against prophecies from the Old Testament.

Chantry Chapel : Also sometimes known as a Chantry, was a chapel set aside as a memorial to a person or family in the medieval period. The wealthy patrons within a church paid to have prayers said daily for them.

Clerestory : Uppermost storey of the walls of a church, pierced by windows.

Decorated style : A phase of English Gothic architecture, named from the elaborate form of window tracery used at this time when simple circular forms of geometric were replaced by more varied patterns. Exeter contains an exceptional variety of forms. The term applies not only to windows but all ecclesiastical art used during the period 1307-1377.

Early English : The first appearance of the pointed arch (Gothic or French influence) in windows during 1189-1307, without elaborate tracery and fewer lights than the Decorated style.

Enamel Paint : Is applied to white glass and fired to fix it, and made from a flux of powdered glass and metal oxides.

Ferramenta : A wrought iron framework to support stained glass, held together with wedges.

Gothic : Style of architecture introduced from France in the medieval period, following the Romanesque period. One of the features is the pointed arch to create larger windows.

Grisaille : From the French meaning greyish, white glass is painted with repetitive foliage patterns in black or brown, without coloured figurative designs.

Iconoclasm : The rejection or destruction of religious images as heretical.

Iconography : The interpretation of visual images and symbols in art.

Isothermal glazing : Environmental protection to deter further corrosion of the glass. A protective glazing system keeps the glass dry on both sides by an extra layer of glass to maintain a similar temperature on both sides of the stained glass, thus stopping condensation occurring on the stained glass, by allowing the air to circulate.

Lancet : A slender pointed arched window. (ie 'lance' shaped).

Lights : The main sections of a window divided by vertical stonework called mullions.

Perpendicular style : The last of the Gothic styles after the Decorated period in 1377, with more vertical mullions and horizontal transoms to create the largest windows seen (e.g. The Great East Window). The period lasted from 1377-1485.

Pot metal glass : Made by mixing appropriate metal oxides with sand and a flux in a crucible and firing until molten to give the stained glass colour throughout.

Quarries : Used as a background to a figure in a window, with usually lozenge or diamond shaped glass pieces, with repeating motifs (birds, fleur-de-lys etc) in silver staining.

Romanesque : The architectural style of medieval Europe. This came to Britain after 1066, as the Norman style but ended roughly in 1200. It is characterised by rounded window arches, small splayed windows, and massive pillars. The twin towers at Exeter are examples of this period.

Roundel : A circular or oval panel or window.

Silver stain : A compound of silver nitrate applied usually to the back of a window, that when fired turns the white glass from pale yellow to orange depending on the conditions. It is often used for a nimbus (halo) or hair, and can be used to turn blue glass green.

Tracery : Describes the use of stone bars or moulding to divide the window into lights. In Decorated Gothic windows it is more specifically used to refer to the ornate patterns of stonework above the main lights, and called tracery lights.

Transepts : Either part of a church or Cathedral that forms the arms of the building, (i.e. cross shaped) projecting usually at right angles from the nave.

Type-antitype : Typological windows are in pairs with an Old Testament event prefiguring aspects found in the New Testament (e.g. Jonah who survived three days in the whale, and the Resurrection of Christ after three days). This is an example of typology or type-antitype events in the Bible.

Vidimus : From Latin meaning 'we saw,' but meaning in stained glass windows a scale diagram of the full window, to attach to the contract for a client to approve.